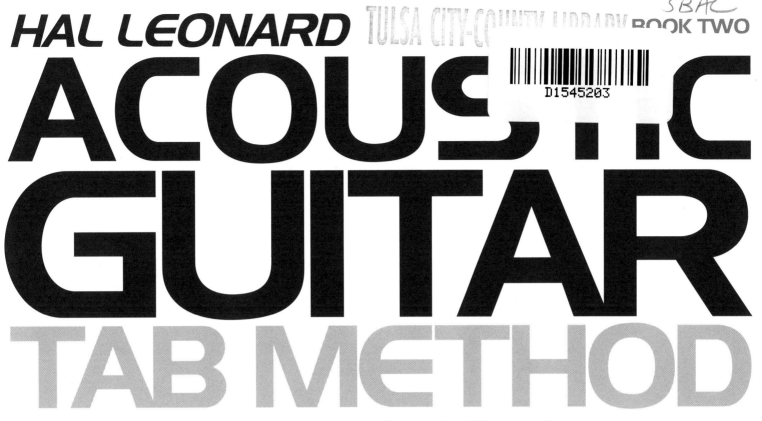

HAL LEONARD
ACOUSTIC GUITAR
TAB METHOD

SBAC
BOOK TWO

D1545203

Written by Michael Mueller and Jeff Schroedl

Editor: Kurt Plahna

2 **The F Chord**
Barre, Chord Diagram

4 **New Rhythms**
Sixteenth Note

6 **Fingerpicking**
6/8 Time

10 **Major Scale**
Whole Steps, Half Steps

13 **Music Theory 101**
Key, Tonic

14 **Add and Sus Chords**
Triads, Scale Degrees, Tonality

18 **Travis Picking**
Downbeat, Slash Chords, Drop D Tuning

22 **Strumming in 6/8**

23 **Using a Capo**
Keys

26 **Minor Pentatonic Scale**
Triplets, Eighth-Note Triplet, Transposed, Shuffle, Palm Muting

28 **Moving Open Chords**
Positions

30 **Open-String Barre Chords**

To access audio visit:
www.halleonard.com/mylibrary

Enter Code
2241-0474-8721-7888

ISBN 978-1-4803-9811-5

HAL•LEONARD®
CORPORATION
7777 W. BLUEMOUND RD. P.O. BOX 13819 MILWAUKEE, WI 53213

Visit Hal Leonard Online at
www.halleonard.com

THE F CHORD

The F chord uses no open strings, and it also requires the use of a **barre** (pronounced "bar"). Barring is done by flattening a finger across more than one string at a time. Here, use your 1st finger to press down the 1st and 2nd strings. Adjust the angle of your finger, or rotate your finger slightly on its side as necessary, so the notes sound clearly. Fret the remaining two notes with your 2nd and 3rd fingers as shown in the **chord diagram** below—a graphic representation of the fretboard often used in guitar notation.

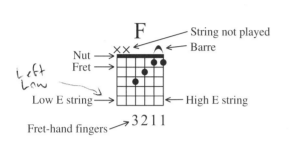

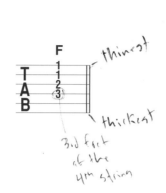

FREE BIRD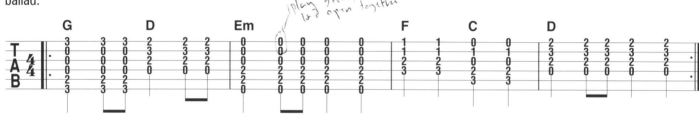

Let's take it slow with your new chord; try playing it in the opening acoustic chord progression of Lynyrd Skynyrd's classic rock ballad.

LOSING MY RELIGION

Now let's try the intro to this R.E.M. classic, which not only features the F chord but also combines single-note licks with strummed chords.

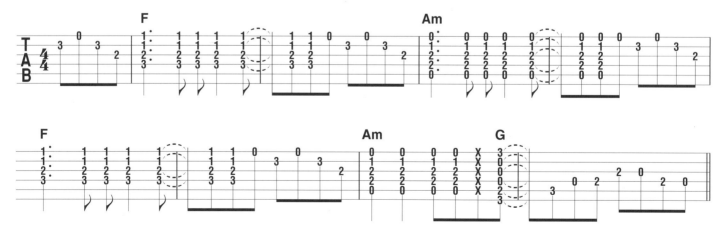

LIKE A ROLLING STONE

Bob Dylan's iconic song is fun to strum. Feel free to vary the strumming rhythm, to find one that feels natural to you.

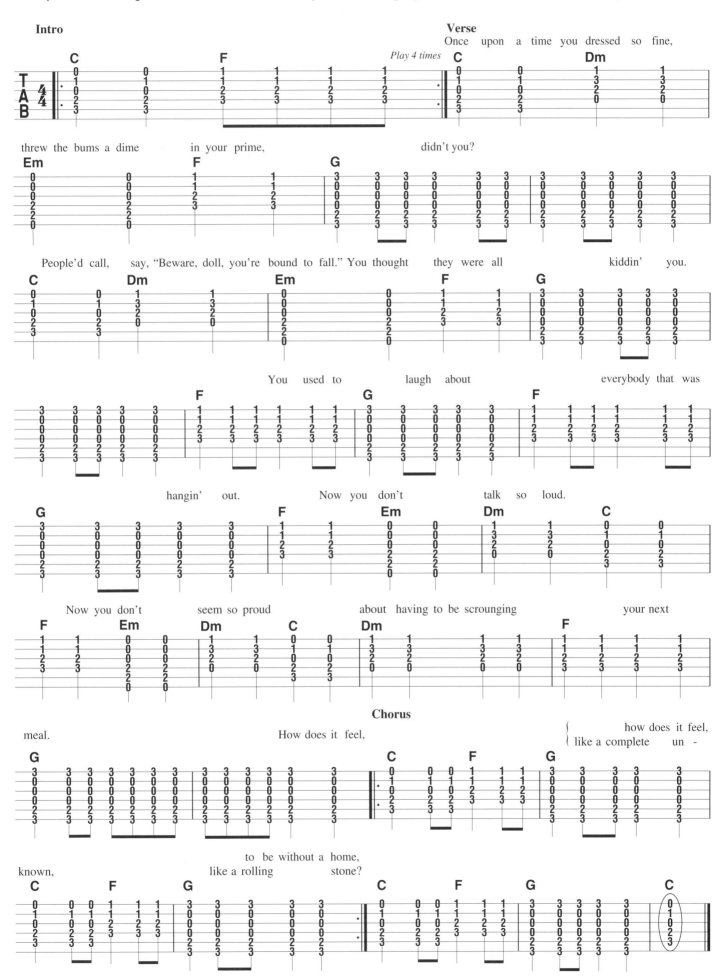

NEW RHYTHMS

A **sixteenth note** lasts half as long as an eighth note and is written with two flags or two beams. There are four sixteenth notes in one beat.

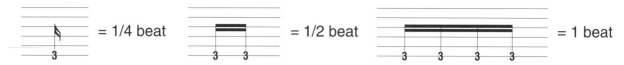

HELTER SKELTER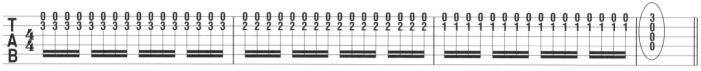

The raucous intro to this song by the Beatles uses sixteenth notes. Divide the beat into four and count "one-e-and-a, two-e-and-a, three-e-and-a, four-e-and-a."

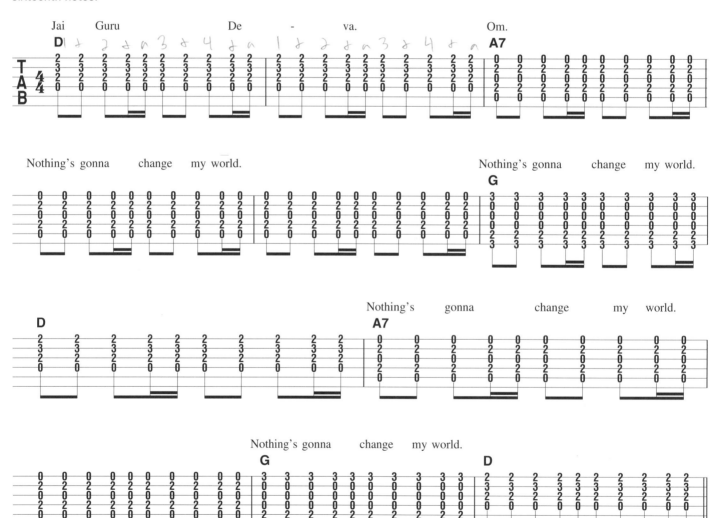

Count: one-e-and-a 2-e-and a etc.

ACROSS THE UNIVERSE

Here's another from the treasure trove that is the Beatles' catalog. The chorus in this tune includes eighth notes mixed with sixteenth notes.

ANGIE

The chorus of this Rolling Stones ballad also mixes eighth- and sixteenth-note strums—a common rhythmic figure.

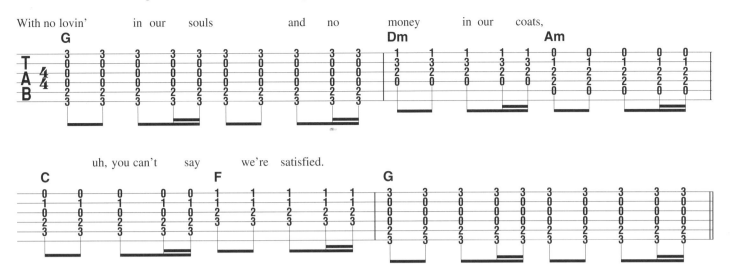

CRAZY ON YOU

Combining an eighth note with two sixteenth notes is commonly called a "gallop" rhythm—one heard famously in Heart's classic rocker "Crazy on You."

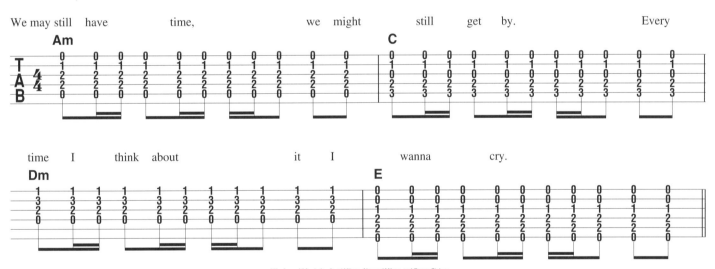

SAVE TONIGHT

Singer-songwriter Eagle-Eye Cherry scored a huge hit with "Save Tonight" in 1998.

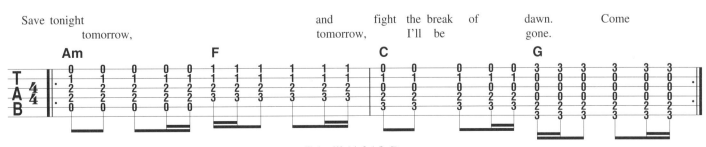

FINGERPICKING

Up to this point, you've been using a pick, or plectrum, to strum chords or play single-note melodies. But one of the most popular ways to play the acoustic guitar is **fingerpicking**, or using your pick hand's fingers to pluck the strings.

Typically, you'll use your thumb, index, middle, and ring fingers in fingerstyle technique, with only rare instances of needing the pinky. Those four digits are labeled using the letters *p*, *i*, *m*, and *a*, respectively.

To get started, here are a couple of exercises for playing ascending and descending finger-picking patterns.

GOING UP

This exercise alternates between C and G chords. On the G chord, you'll need to skip the 5th string.

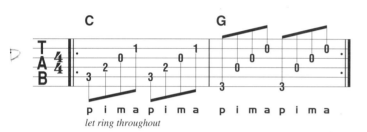

GOING DOWN

And now we descend the same two arpeggios. Remember to keep your ring, middle, and index fingers over strings 2, 3, and 4, respectively, shifting only your thumb between the 5th and 6th strings.

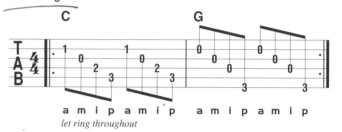

The next two examples are in **6/8 time**, which means there are six eighth notes per measure. The pulse of this time signature is generally felt in two beats, each containing three eighth notes, so it may be helpful to count each measure as **1**-2-3-**4**-5-6 or **1**-2-3, **2**-2-3. You'll learn more about 6/8 time on page 22.

NOTHING ELSE MATTERS

This opening riff on Em is a great primer.

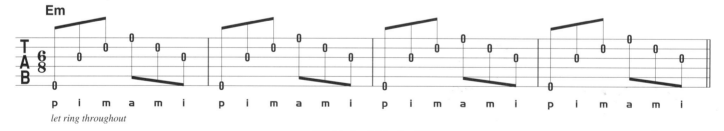

EVERYBODY HURTS

R.E.M.'s melancholy ballad is built on a simple D–G arpeggio riff.

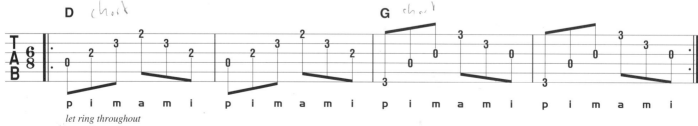

In Book One, you learned all of the notes within the first five frets. The next two fingerpicking examples take you "up the neck," beyond first position. Follow the tab, and you'll be fine. But knowing the actual note names will only help in the long run, so here are the notes within frets 5–12 on all six strings.

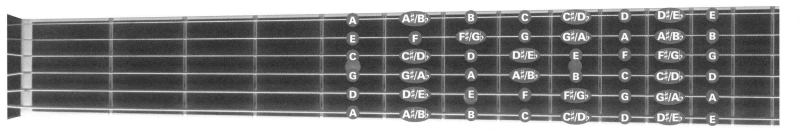

SILENT LUCIDITY

The cascading arpeggio riff in this Queensrÿche ballad requires only your thumb, index, and middle fingers, though you'll need to shift across string sets.

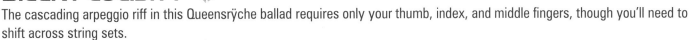

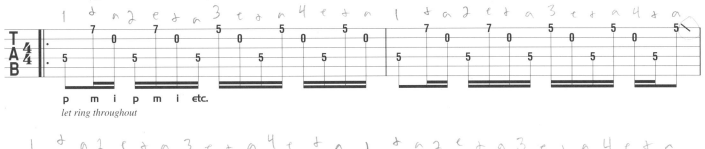

WHEN THE CHILDREN CRY

Similar to "Silent Lucidity," White Lion's smash ballad pits high-register fretted notes on the top E string against open B and G strings. It also introduces your first simultaneous plucking of the low and high E strings. Use your thumb on the low E string and your ring finger on the high one.

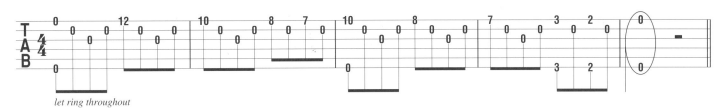

In addition to strictly ascending and descending arpeggios, you will also employ the fingerpicking technique on nonadjacent string patterns. In other words, rather than playing p–i–m–a or its reverse, you need to be able to play patterns such as the following.

P–M–I–A

This is one of the most popular fingerpicking patterns.

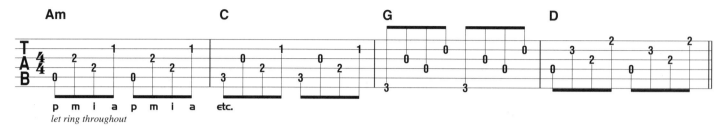

P–I–A–M

Here is another common pattern.

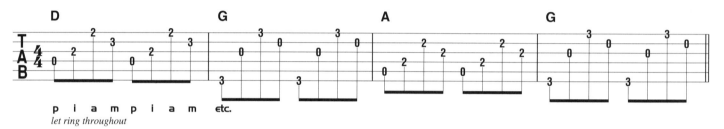

WHO WILL SAVE YOUR SOUL

Jewel's 1995 hit expands on the p–m–i–a exercise above, requiring you to play two consecutive notes on the same string. Try using the suggested fingering.

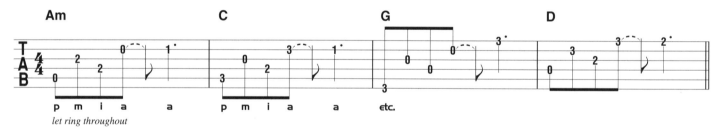

ANNIE'S SONG

The intro to John Denver's "Annie's Song" uses the p–i–a–m pattern, with a repeat of the a–m portion

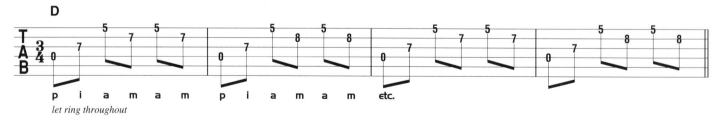

HALLELUJAH

Widely regarded as one of the greatest songs ever written, this Leonard Cohen classic has been famously covered by such greats as k.d. lang, Rufus Wainwright, and, of course, Jeff Buckley. Note the alternative voicings for the G and Em chords (technically, Em7). Hold down the 3rd fret of strings 1 and 2 for both chords.

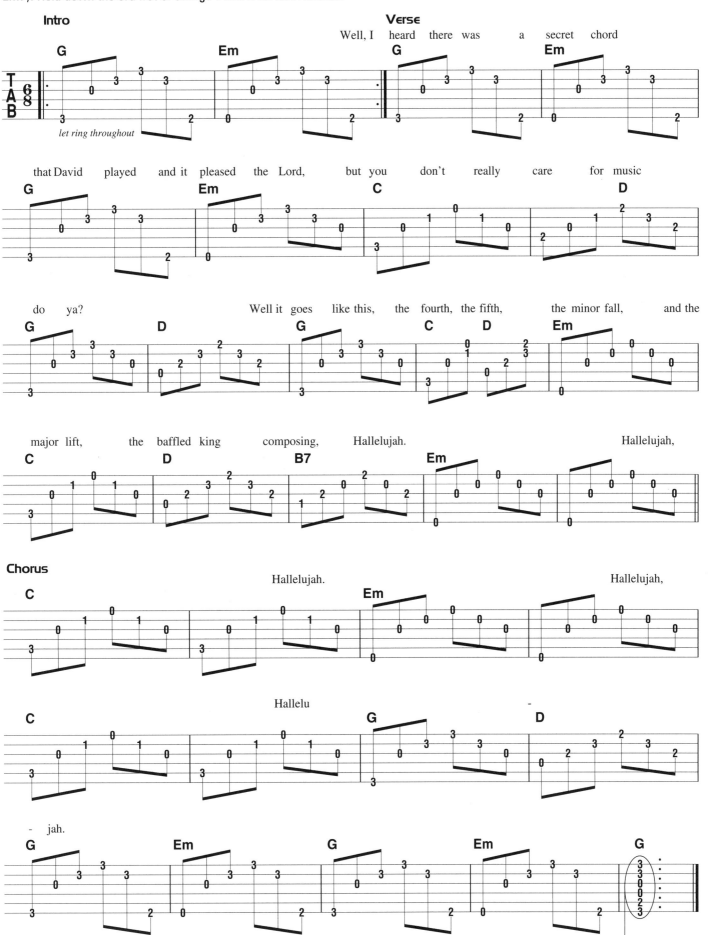

THE MAJOR SCALE

A **scale** is a succession of notes ascending or descending in a specific order. The most common scale is the **major scale**. It can be built starting on any root note, and follows a specific pattern of **whole steps** (two frets) and **half steps** (one fret). Here it is beginning on the low E.

E MAJOR SCALE

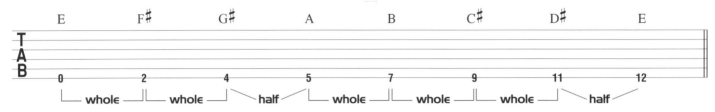

Although it's easy to visualize the scale pattern across one string, it's not practical to play it this way. Here is the standard fingering for the major scale on the guitar.

G MAJOR SCALE

The scale above starts on the note G, so it's a G major scale. If you move the pattern up two frets, it becomes an A major scale.

A MAJOR SCALE

You can apply this movable major scale pattern to any root note along the low string. Practice this pattern using alternate picking and in both ascending and descending direction.

Here's another way to visualize the movable pattern:

Major Scale Pattern 1 – Root on 6th String

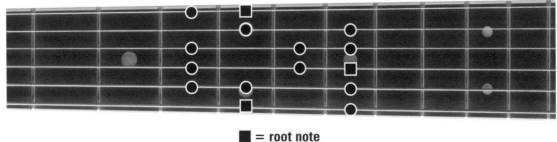

■ = root note

Practicing scales is a good way to develop fret-hand technique. Start slowly and gradually build up speed.

The notes of the major scale are the foundation for countless melodies, riffs, solos, and chord progressions. Here are a few examples.

DO-RE-MI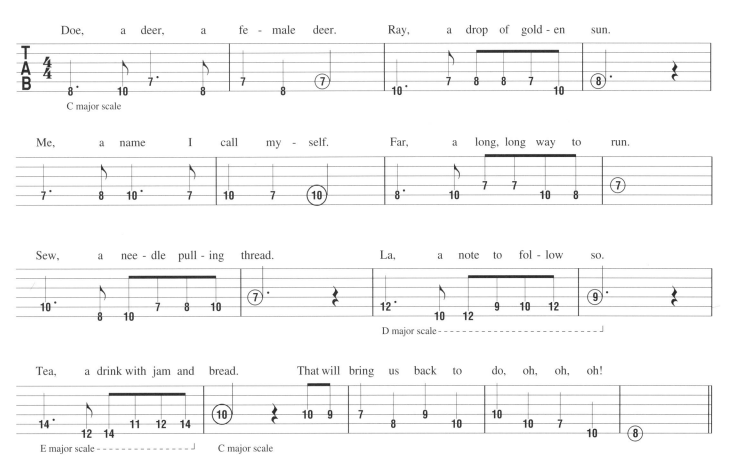

This Rodgers and Hammerstein song from *The Sound of Music* is arguably the most famous use of the major scale in popular music. The lyrics also teach the seven solfège syllables commonly used to sing the major scale. The melody uses mostly notes from the C major scale, and shifts briefly to D major and E major in measures 11 and 13, respectively.

from THE SOUND OF MUSIC
Lyrics by Oscar Hammerstein II
Music by Richard Rodgers
Copyright © 1959 by Richard Rodgers and Oscar Hammerstein II
Copyright Renewed
Williamson Music, a Division of Rodgers & Hammerstein: an Imagem Company, owner of publication and allied rights throughout the world

HELLO, GOODBYE

The main riff in the chorus of this song by the Beatles runs straight up the C major scale, tabbed here in open position.

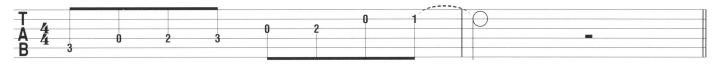

Words and Music by John Lennon and Paul McCartney
Copyright © 1967 Sony/ATV Music Publishing LLC
Copyright Renewed
All Rights Administered by Sony/ATV Music Publishing LLC, 424 Church Street, Suite 1200, Nashville, TN 37219

There are many patterns for playing the major scale on the guitar. Here's one with three notes per string that has its root on the 5th string. Let's try it in D.

D MAJOR SCALE

To help you visualize the pattern, here it is on the fretboard:

Major Scale Pattern 2 – Root on 5th String

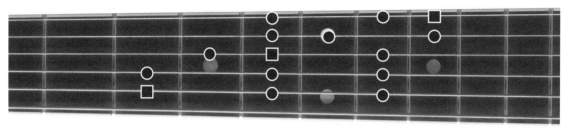

■ = root note

JOY TO THE WORLD 🔊

The melody of this famous Christmas carol, by Baroque composer George Frideric Handel, uses all of the notes in the D major scale.

MUSIC THEORY 101

When we see that the notes of a particular song come from a certain scale, we say that the song is in the **key** of that scale. For instance, if the notes of a song all come from the C major scale, we say that the song is in the key of C major.

GOODBYE TO ROMANCE

The intro to "Goodbye to Romance" by Ozzy Osbourne uses notes exclusively from the D major scale:

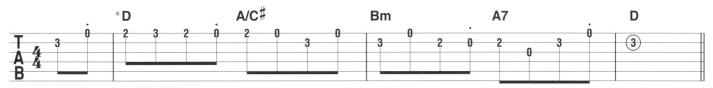

*Chord symbols for reference only.

Words and Music by John Osbourne, Robert Daisley and Randy Rhoads
TRO - © Copyright 1981 and 1984 Essex Music International, Inc., New York and Blizzard Music, Daytona Beach, FL

Notice how the guitar part seems to be "at rest" when you arrive at the last note (D)? This is because the D note is the root, or **tonic**—the note around which the key revolves.

MAJOR SCALE CHART

Major scales are the building blocks of music, and music theory. Chords and chord progressions are also derived from scales. Following is a handy table that spells the notes in all 12 keys. Don't get bogged down trying to memorize all this at once, but you might want to dog-ear this page for future reference.

	1 (root)	2	3	4	5	6	7
C major	C	D	E	F	G	A	B
G major	G	A	B	C	D	E	F♯
D major	D	E	F♯	G	A	B	C♯
A major	A	B	C♯	D	E	F♯	G♯
E major	E	F♯	G♯	A	B	C♯	D♯
B major	B	C♯	D♯	E	F♯	G♯	A♯
F♯ major	F♯	G♯	A♯	B	C♯	D♯	E♯
D♭ major	D♭	E♭	F	G♭	A♭	B♭	C
A♭ major	A♭	B♭	C	D♭	E♭	F	G
E♭ major	E♭	F	G	A♭	B♭	C	D
B♭ major	B♭	C	D	E♭	F	G	A
F major	F	G	A	B♭	C	D	E

ADD & SUS CHORDS

The major chords (or **triads**) you've learned so far comprise three notes, or **scale degrees**—the root, 3rd, and 5th. In this section, we're going to show you how to alter these triads either by addition or by substitution.

ADD CHORDS

An **add** chord is just what it sounds like—a triad with a fourth note added to it. Typically, the 2nd (or 9th) note of the chord's attendant scale is the added note, with the 4th (or 11th) also occasionally used.

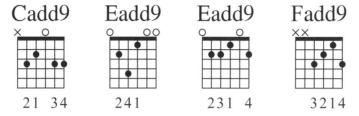

A HARD DAY'S NIGHT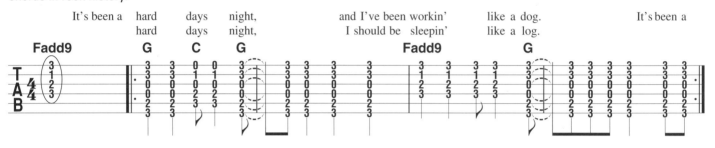

The Fadd9 that George Harrison struck on his 12-string guitar as the opening salvo to this Beatles hit is one of the most famous chords in rock history.

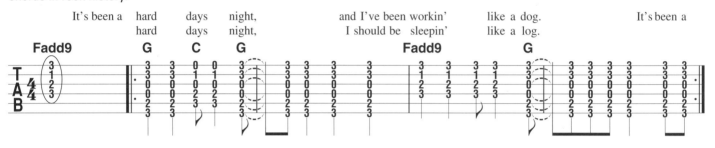

Probably the most popular add chord is the Cadd9 with the pinky fretting the high E string at the 3rd fret, and it typically follows or precedes the similarly configured G chord.

3 AM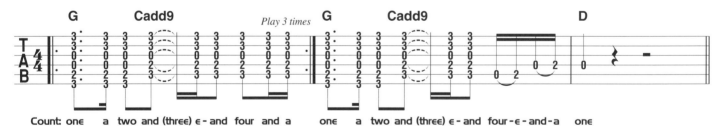

"3 AM," which epitomizes the G–Cadd9 progression, was a huge hit for modern rockers Matchbox 20 in the mid-'90s. This song also features a new rhythm: a dotted eighth note followed by a sixteenth note. Follow the count below the staff and listen to the audio track to get a feel for it.

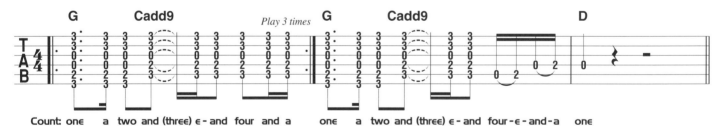

I REMEMBER YOU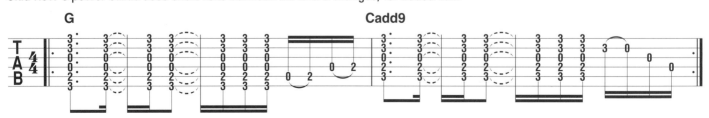

Skid Row's power ballad uses short licks between the chord changes, for added flair.

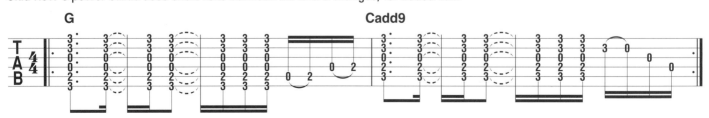

SUS CHORDS

In a triad, the 3rd degree determines whether it's major or minor in **tonality** (or quality). So if you remove the 3rd degree and instead play the 2nd or 4th in its place, you "suspend" the chord's tonality. This is called a **sus** chord.

The most common sus chords are built on open D and A chords.

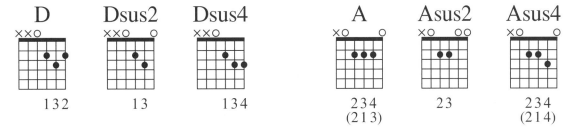

TAKE A PICTURE

Filter's smash 2000 hit features Asus2 and Dsus4 chords. Notice the open-string strum on the final eighth note of measures 2 and 4. This is a technique often used in strumming, to allow you ample time to change chords.

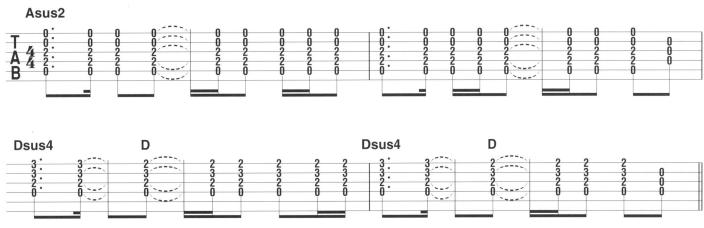

BEHIND BLUE EYES

Pete Townshend's beautiful acoustic intro to "Behind Blue Eyes" is built upon an Esus4 chord. Fret an E major chord, then place your pinky finger on the 2nd fret of the 3rd string, and you've got the chord.

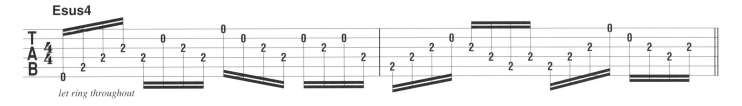

let ring throughout

CLOSER TO FINE

In this Indigo Girls hit, you'll see the popular Dsus4–D–Dsus2–D move as well as a new chord: A7sus4. This is simply a Cadd9 shape, but with an open A string instead of the 3rd fret C note.

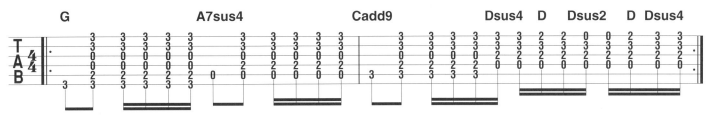

EVERY ROSE HAS ITS THORN

Poison's smash ballad is built upon the ubiquitous G–Cadd9 progression. A strum pattern is provided for the intro; use variations of that for the verses and chorus. Once you've reached the end of the interlude, you'll see the instructions "D.S. al Coda." Jump back to the sign (𝄋) at the verse and play up to the instruction "To Coda." At this point, jump to the last line of the tune where it's labeled "Coda," and play the final measures.

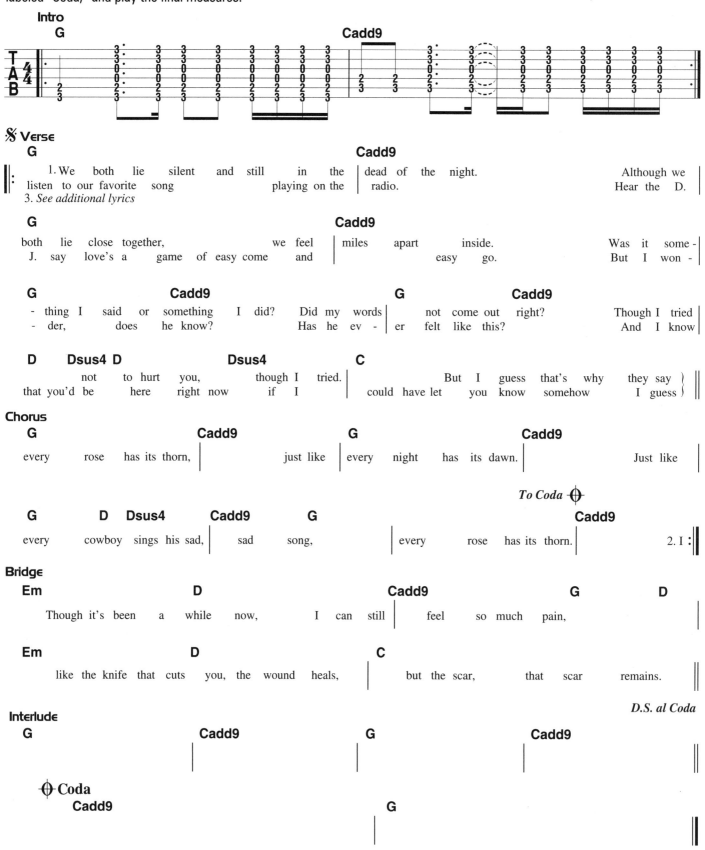

Additional Lyrics

3. I know I could have saved our love that night if I'd known what to say.
   Instead of making love we both made our separate ways.
   And now I hear you've found somebody new, and that I never meant that much to you.
   To hear that tears me up inside, and to see you cuts me like a knife.

Words and Music by Bobby Dall, C.C. Deville, Bret Michaels and Rikki Rockett
Copyright © 1988 by Cyanide Publishing
All Rights in the United States Administered by Universal Music - Z Songs

WONDERWALL

Oasis crafted an alternative-rock standard with their 1995 hit "Wonderwall." This song features a D–G drone on the top two strings, including the A7sus4 chord you already learned and a new chord called Em7; check out the tab to see how to play it.

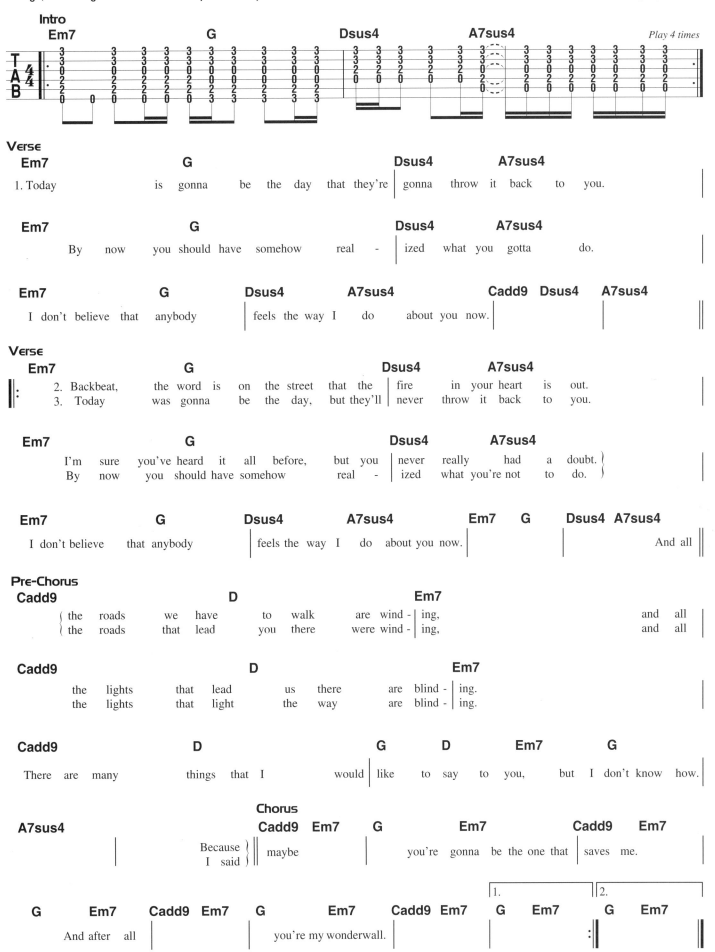

Words and Music by Noel Gallagher
Copyright © 1995 SM Music Publishing UK Limited and Oasis Music
All Rights Administered by Sony/ATV Music Publishing LLC, 424 Church Street, Suite 1200, Nashville, TN 37219

TRAVIS PICKING

Named for legendary country artist Merle Travis and perfected by the original "Certified Guitar Player" Chet Atkins, the **Travis picking** technique has become an essential element of playing acoustic guitar. What sets Travis picking apart from regular finger-picking is its use of alternating bass notes plucked by the thumb. Throughout this section, you'll see a variety of chords that you haven't encountered yet, as well as new voicings for chords you already know. By this point, you should be able to tackle new chords without too much difficulty. Simply follow the rhythm tab and keep on pickin'!

BASIC TRAVIS STYLE

Here is a very basic form of Travis picking. Pay attention to the fingering instructions. Notice how your thumb always plucks a note on the **downbeat** (beats 1, 2, 3, or 4). This is almost always the case in Travis picking.

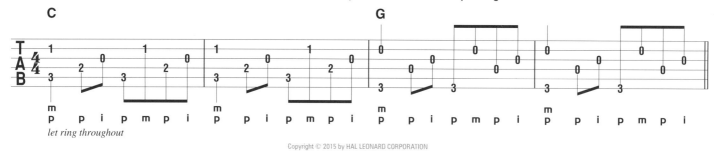

TRAVIS VARIATIONS

In this riff, your thumb plays notes on all three lower strings; use your pick hand's ring finger for notes on the high E string.

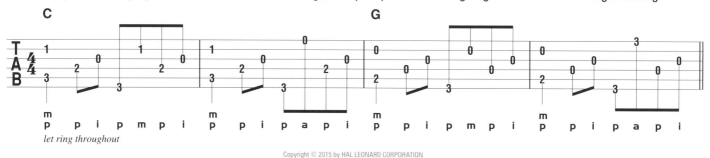

YOU WERE MEANT FOR ME

Alaskan singer-songwriter Jewel reached #2 on the Billboard charts with this Travis-picked 1996 folk-pop ballad. Check out the new sus chord—a Csus2 that utilizes the open D string.

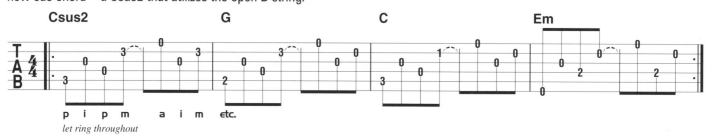

Words and Music by Jewel Murray and Steve Poltz
© 1995, 1996 WIGGLY TOOTH MUSIC and THIRD STORY MUSIC, INC.
All Rights for WIGGLY TOOTH MUSIC Administered by DCTM AVE/DOWNTOWN MUSIC PUBLISHING LLC
Worldwide Rights for THIRD STORY MUSIC, INC. owned by ARC/CONRAD MUSIC LLC
All Rights for ARC/CONRAD MUSIC LLC Administered by BMG RIGHTS MANAGEMENT (US) LLC

JULIA

John Lennon's ode to his mother is a perfect example of the beauty Travis picking can produce. The progression features variations on the C and Em chords, plus a new chord: Am7. All three chords include the high G note on the 3rd fret of the 1st string. Keep it fretted with your pinky throughout the entire passage.

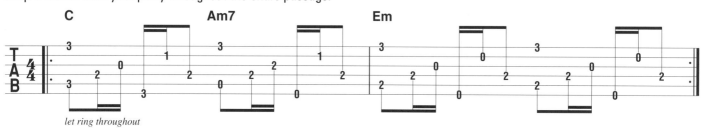

Words and Music by John Lennon and Paul McCartney
Copyright © 1968 Sony/ATV Music Publishing LLC
Copyright Renewed
All Rights Administered by Sony/ATV Music Publishing LLC, 424 Church Street, Suite 1200, Nashville, TN 37219

TAKE ME HOME, COUNTRY ROADS

John Denver's signature track is one of the most beloved folk songs of all time.

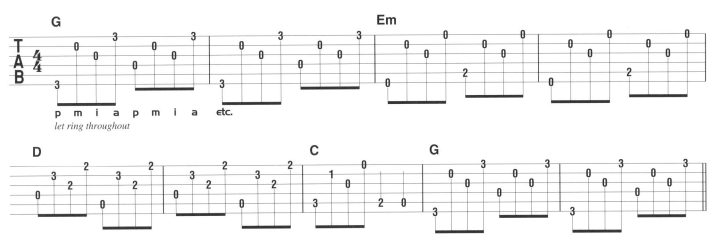

Words and Music by John Denver, Bill Danoff and Taffy Nivert
Copyright © 1971; Renewed 1999 BMG Ruby Songs, Anna Kate Deutschendorf, Zachary Deutschendorf, BMG Rights Management (Ireland) Ltd. and Jesse Belle Denver in the U.S.
All Rights for BMG Ruby Songs, Anna Kate Deutschendorf and Zachary Deutschendorf Administered by BMG Rights Management (US) LLC
All Rights for BMG Rights Management (Ireland) Ltd. Administered by Chrysalis One Music
All Rights for Jesse Belle Denver Administered by WB Music Corp.

CAN'T FIND MY WAY HOME

Steve Winwood's verse riff features a device commonly found in Travis picking: a descending bass line. You'll see **slash chords** above the staff, in which the notes shown to the right of each slash are the bass notes of the chords—in this case, moving down by half steps.

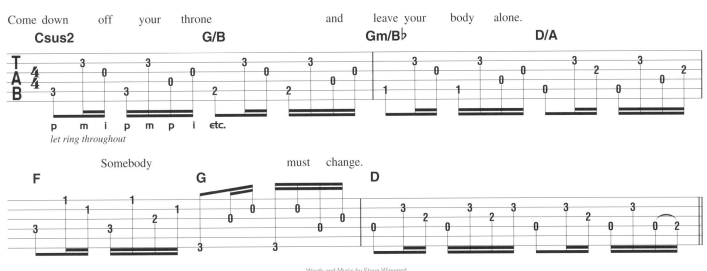

Words and Music by Steve Winwood
© 1970 (Renewed) F.S. MUSIC LTD.
All Rights Administered by WARNER-TAMERLANE PUBLISHING CORP.

DEAR PRUDENCE

This Beatles classic not only features a descending bass line but also requires you to tune your low E string down one whole step, to D. This is called **drop D tuning**. For the D7 chord, use your pinky to fret the 3rd fret of the 5th string while holding down the D chord shape.

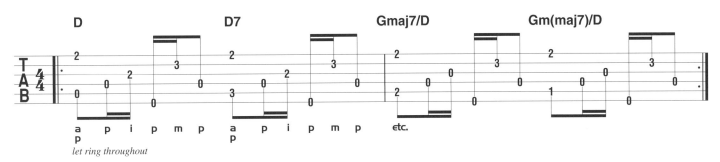

Words and Music by John Lennon and Paul McCartney
Copyright © 1968 Sony/ATV Music Publishing LLC
Copyright Renewed
All Rights Administered by Sony/ATV Music Publishing LLC, 424 Church Street, Suite 1200, Nashville, TN 37219

DUST IN THE WIND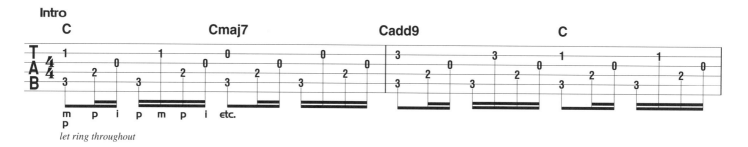

This timeless piece from progressive rockers Kansas is arguably the most popular acoustic Travis picking song in rock history.

Intro

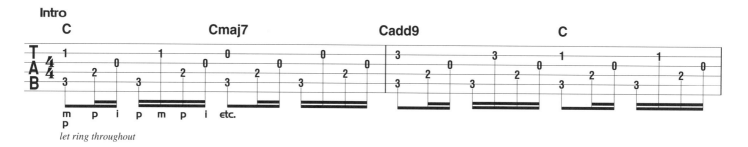

let ring throughout

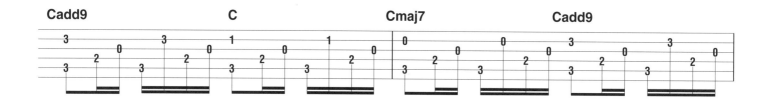

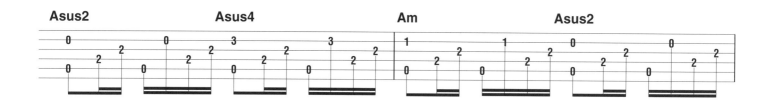

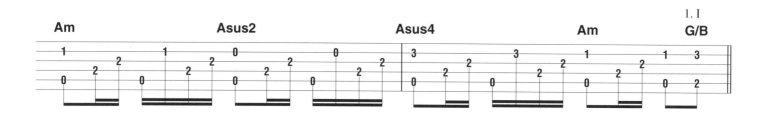

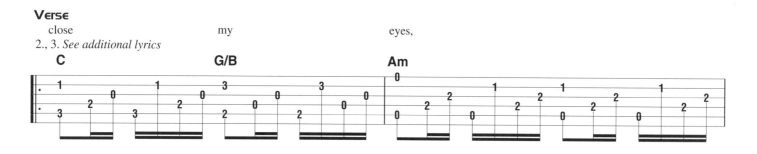

Verse

close   my   eyes,

2., 3. See additional lyrics

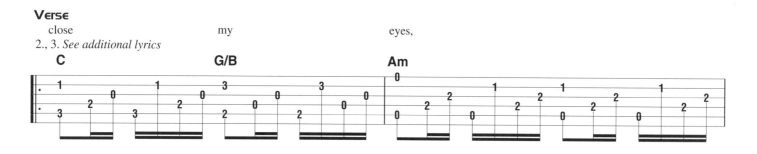

only   for   a moment,   and   the   moment's gone.

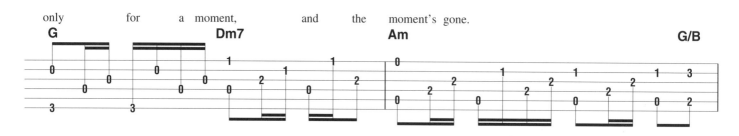

Words and Music by Kerry Livgren
© 1977 (Renewed 2005), 1978 EMI BLACKWOOD MUSIC INC. and DON KIRSHNER MUSIC
All Rights Controlled and Administered by EMI BLACKWOOD MUSIC INC.

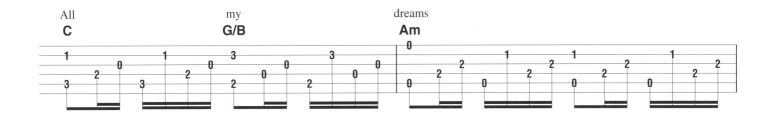

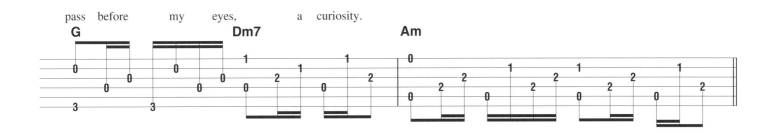

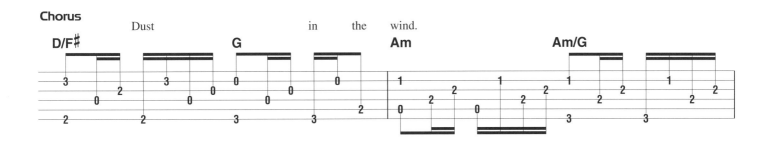

Chorus

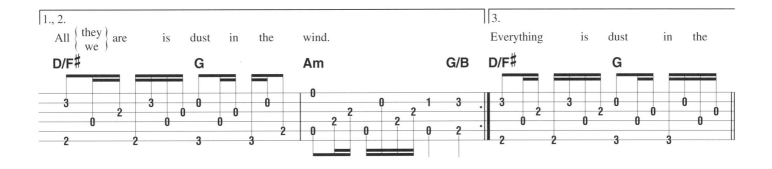

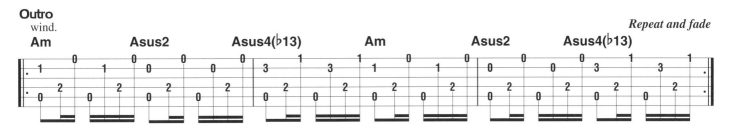

Outro

Repeat and fade

Additional Lyrics

2. Same old song.
   Just a drop of water in an endless sea.
   All we do
   Crumbles to the ground though we refuse to see.

3. Don't hang on,
   Nothing lasts forever but the earth and sky.
   It slips away
   And all your money won't another minute buy.

STRUMMING IN 6/8

Earlier in this book (page 6), you played a couple of songs containing arpeggios set in 6/8. Now let's look at the 6/8 time signature in greater depth. As mentioned previously, the 6/8 time signature indicates six eighth notes per measure, with a pulse typically felt in two beats.

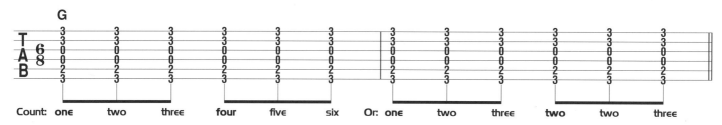

One place you commonly hear the 6/8 pulse is in an Irish jig. Though you strum in a **1**–2–3–**4**–5–6 pattern during a jig, there is a quirk of the style, in that you strum it in a down-up-down, down-up-down pattern. Those consecutive downstrokes can be a bit tricky at first, but they're key to authentic Irish accompaniment.

THE IRISH WASHERWOMAN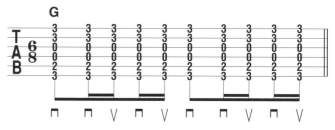

Follow the downstroke (⊓) and upstroke (∨) symbols below the staff.

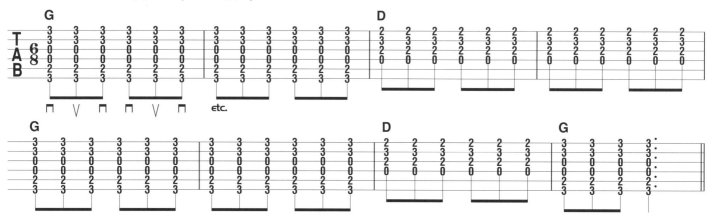

Here are a couple of commonly heard 6/8 strum patterns.

6/8 VARIATION 1 🔊

This strum pattern doubles up on beats 2 and 5 using 16th-note strums.

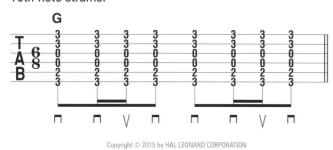

6/8 VARIATION 2 🔊

This strum pattern takes the last one a step further, adding 16th-note strums to beats 2, 3, 5, and 6.

THE HOUSE OF THE RISING SUN 🔊

The Animals' 1964 hit features one of the all-time great rock arpeggio riffs in 6/8 time.

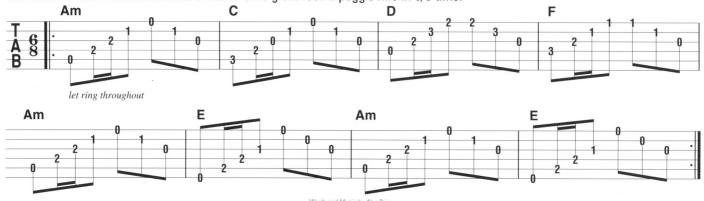

USING A CAPO

A **capo** is a device that clamps around your guitar's neck to raise the pitch of the strings, in effect, creating a new "open position." For example, if you place a capo across the 2nd fret, and then play an open D chord, you're actually sounding an E chord. The main advantage of using a capo on acoustic guitar is that it allows you to play open chords in keys that don't always permit it.

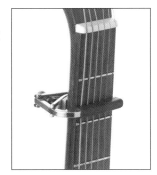

As you play through the following examples using a capo, note that chords are named and tabs numbered respective to the capo; that is, if you're playing an open C shape in front of the capo at the 4th fret, you're sounding an E chord, but we still call it C.

FADE INTO YOU

Mazzy Star scored one of the most memorable hits of the early 1990s with this 6/8 strummer. Place a capo at the 2nd fret.

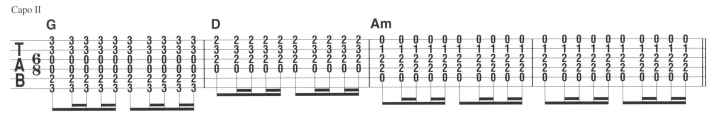

KISS FROM A ROSE

This 1994 Seal hit in 6/8 time requires a capo at the 3rd fret.

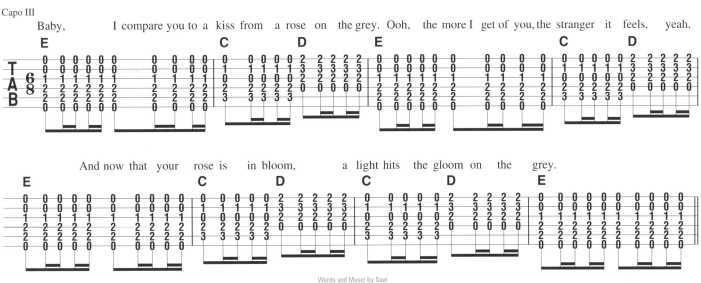

WALK ON THE OCEAN

Toad the Wet Sprocket scored a 1991 alt-rock hit with "Walk on the Ocean." Place your capo at the 4th fret to play in its original key.

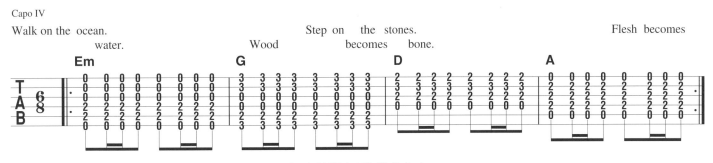

NORWEGIAN WOOD (THIS BIRD HAS FLOWN)

The Beatles embraced their British folk DNA on "Norwegian Wood (This Bird Has Flown)," which was also the first pop song to feature electric sitar. Place a capo at the 2nd fret to play this one. Important tip: while holding down the open D chord, use your fret hand's pinky finger to play the notes at the 4th fret in the intro and verse sections.

Capo II

Intro

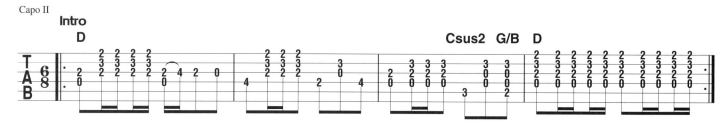

Verse

1. I once had a girl, or should I say she once had me.

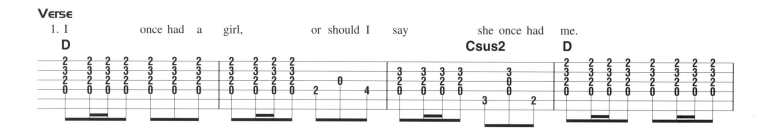

She showed me her room, isn't it good, Norwegian Wood? She

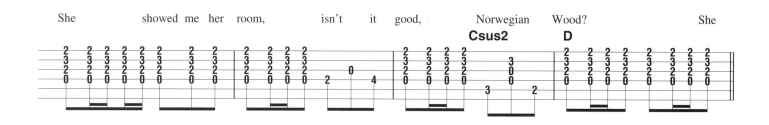

𝄋 Bridge

asked me to stay and she told me to sit any - where. So

See additional lyrics

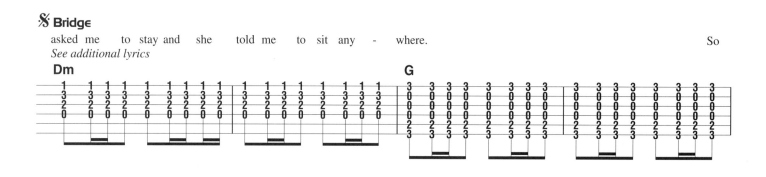

I looked around and I noticed there wasn't a chair.

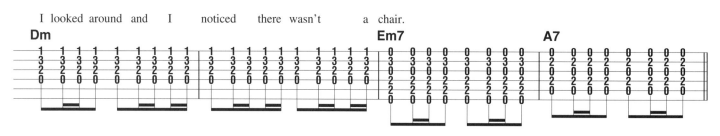

Words and Music by John Lennon and Paul McCartney
Copyright © 1965 Sony/ATV Music Publishing LLC
Copyright Renewed
All Rights Administered by Sony/ATV Music Publishing LLC, 424 Church Street, Suite 1200, Nashville, TN 37219

Verse

2. I   sat   on the   rug   biding my time,   drinking her wine.

3. *See additional lyrics*

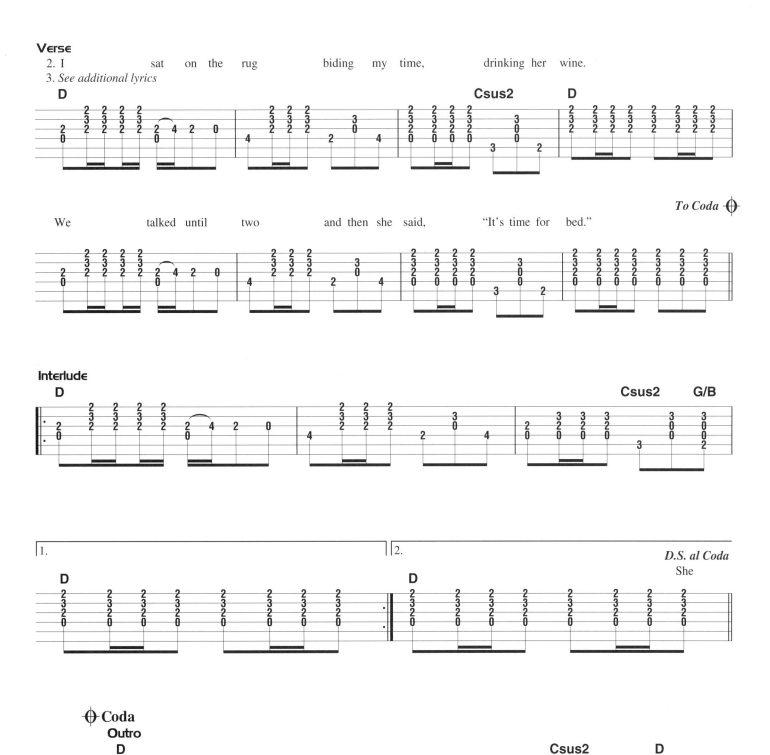

Additional Lyrics

Bridge   She told me she worked in the morning and started to laugh.
              I told her I didn't and crawled off to sleep in the bath.

3. And when I awoke I was alone; this bird had flown.
    So, I lit a fire. Isn't it good Norwegian Wood?

MINOR PENTATONIC SCALE

Earlier, you learned the major scale, which comprises the basic building blocks of popular music. But perhaps the most commonly used scale for riffs, licks, and solos is a five-note scale called the **minor pentatonic scale**.

Here is the E minor pentatonic scale as it appears in open position. Play the notes at the 2nd fret with your middle finger and the notes at the 3rd fret with your ring finger.

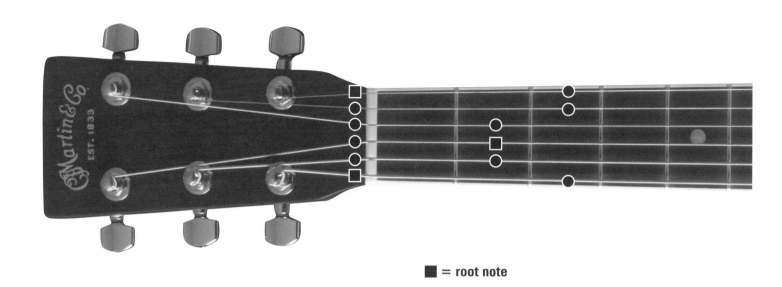

■ = root note

This minor pentatonic pattern is especially popular in acoustic lead guitar settings, because of its open strings. Here are some basic and useful acoustic licks from the E minor pentatonic scale.

LICK #1 🔊

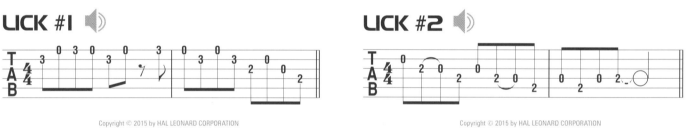

Copyright © 2015 by HAL LEONARD CORPORATION

LICK #2 🔊

Copyright © 2015 by HAL LEONARD CORPORATION

A **triplet** is a group of three notes played in the space of two. Whereas eighth notes divide a beat into two parts, **eighth-note triplets** divide a beat into three parts. They are commonly counted as either "trip-uh-let, trip-uh-let" or "one-and-uh, two-and-uh," and so forth. Triplets are very common in bluesy acoustic licks, like these.

LICK #3 🔊

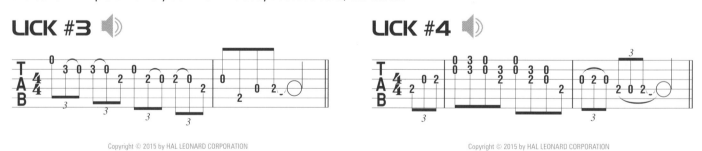

Copyright © 2015 by HAL LEONARD CORPORATION

LICK #4 🔊

Copyright © 2015 by HAL LEONARD CORPORATION

THEORY TIP

The minor pentatonic scale is built from the root, flat-3rd, 4th, 5th, and flat-7th degrees of the major scale.

C major scale =	C	D	E	F	G	A	B
	1		**♭3**	**4**	**5**		**♭7**
C minor pentatonic scale =	C		E♭	F	G		B♭

The minor pentatonic pattern can be **transposed**, or moved up and down the neck to be played in any key. If you start the pattern with your first finger on the 5th fret (low A note), you're playing an A minor pentatonic scale. If you move down to the 1st fret (low F note), it's F minor pentatonic.

A MINOR PENTATONIC

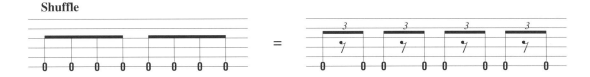

Fret-hand fingers: 1 4 1 3 1 3 1 3 1 4 1 4

F MINOR PENTATONIC

A **shuffle** is a bouncy, skipping rhythm. Eighth notes are played as long-short, rather than as equal values. The feel is the same as inserting a rest in the middle of a triplet. In fact, you've already played the shuffle on a few earlier examples in the book.

BREAKDOWN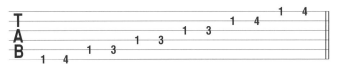

This Tom Petty hit was originally recorded on electric guitar, but it also sounds great in an acoustic arrangement. Play the eighth notes with a shuffle feel.

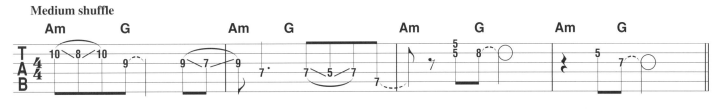

BLACK VELVET

Alannah Myles reached #1 on the charts in 1990 with this bluesy smash. As you play the shuffled eighth notes in measures 2 and 3, use the side or heel of your pick hand to muffle the strings. This technique is called **palm muting** (P.M.).

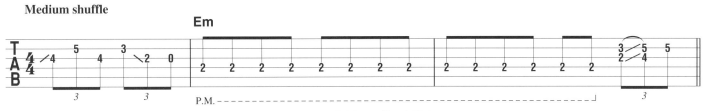

MOVING OPEN CHORDS

Because the acoustic guitar shines particularly brightly when open strings are used, moving open chords around the fretboard while allowing the shape's open strings to ring freely is a popular technique. To determine where an open chord should be moved, we use **positions**. A fretboard position corresponds to the lowest-numbered fret within a chord shape; for example, if you slide the entire open C chord shape up two frets, your index finger will be at the 3rd fret, your middle finger on the 4th, and your ring finger on the 5th, so you would say the chord is in 3rd position.

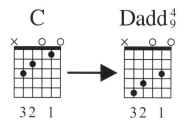

Another thing to keep in mind when sliding open chords around the neck is that you sometimes end up with some pretty crazy chord names, like Dadd9/add11. You don't need to worry about how those names are constructed right now. Just use your ear to determine in which positions the various open chords sound cool.

MAN ON THE MOON

The verse riff of R.E.M.'s "Man on the Moon" comprises an open C chord shape that moves up and down two frets.

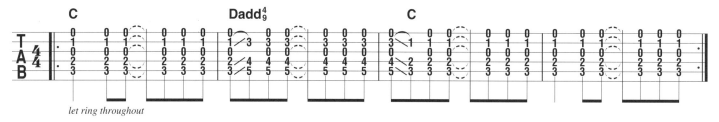

let ring throughout

FLAMENCO IN E

This is a classic flamenco guitar progression in which the open E major chord is slid up to 2nd and 4th positions.

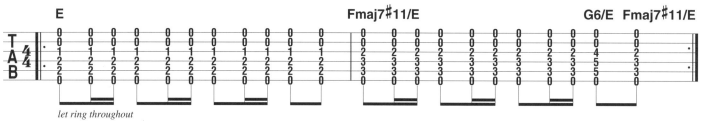

let ring throughout

HOLE HEARTED

Extreme guitarist Nuno Bettencourt is best known for his flashy electric technique, but on this 1991 hit, he shows off his stellar acoustic chops.

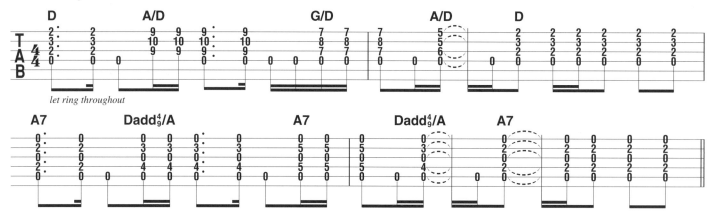

let ring throughout

STAY

Lisa Loeb used a capo at the 6th fret on her 1994 indie smash "Stay."

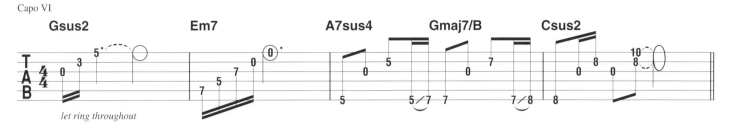

EVERY LITTLE BIT

Patty Griffin's 1996 album *Living with Ghosts* is an emotional thrill ride and a great example of getting the most out of simple chords—like moving an open G chord up and down the neck.

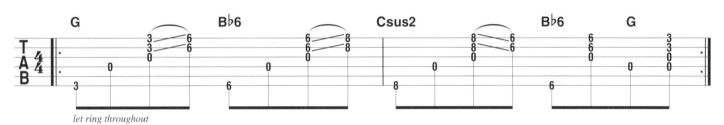

RIDIN' THE STORM OUT

REO Speedwagon guitarist Gary Richrath crafted a classic riff using movable open Am and A chord shapes.

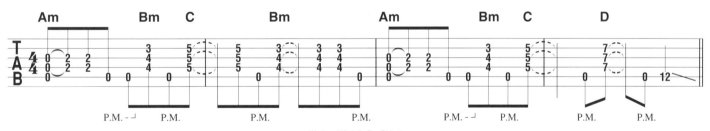

BREAKING THE GIRL

John Frusciante shows off his chordal creativity in the intro and main riff of this Red Hot Chili Peppers classic. Take some time to absorb this tricky 6/8 rhythm, and listen to the audio track for help.

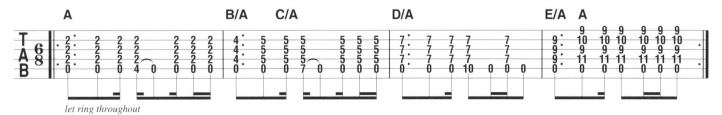

OPEN-STRING BARRE CHORDS

Barre chords are nothing more than open chords moved up the neck, but with your index finger laid across multiple strings in a "bar-like" fashion, acting as a capo. This is a difficult yet necessary technique, but we're going to start with an alternative approach popular among acoustic guitarists.

The following chords are based on popular barre chord shapes, only without the "barre" part. Instead, we're going to allow one or more open strings to ring, which results in a much more colorful chord. As with the moving open chords covered earlier, this practice will yield some rather strange chord names. But again, don't worry about those for now.

Here are the recommended open-string barre chords. You can try others, but they may sound quite dissonant and, frankly, unpleasant!

6th-String Roots

	Fmaj7#11	F#11	G6	Aadd9	Badd11	Cmaj7	D$_9^6$
	0	0	0	0	0	0	0
	0	0	0	0	0	0	0
	2	3	4	6	8	9	11
	3	4	5	7	9	10	12
	3	4	5	7	9	10	12
	1	2	3	5	7	8	10

5th-String Roots

	Bsus4	Cmaj7	C#m7	D$_{add6}^{sus2}$	E5	Fmaj7#11(no3rd)	F#11(no3rd)	G6
	0	0	0	0	0	0	0	0
	0	0	0	0	0	0	0	0
	4	5	6	7	9	10	11	12
	4	5	6	7	9	10	11	12
	2	3	4	5	7	8	9	10

5th-String Roots (alternative voicings)

	Bm(add$_{b6}^{4}$)	C	Dadd$_9^4$	Em	Fmaj9	G6	Am7
	0	0	0	0	0	0	0
	3	5	7	8	10	12	13
	0	0	0	0	0	0	0
	4	5	7	9	10	12	14
	2	3	5	7	8	10	12

KILLER OF GIANTS

Ozzy Osbourne guitarist Jake E. Lee made great use of arpeggiated open-string barre chords in the intro of this track from *The Ultimate Sin*.

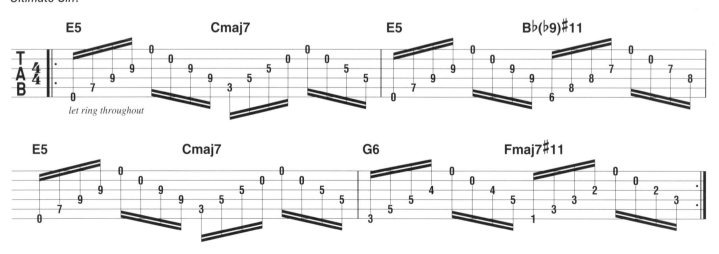

Words and Music by Ozzy Osbourne, Robert Daisley and Jake E. Lee
© 1986 EMI VIRGIN MUSIC LTD.
All Rights for the U.S.A. and Canada Controlled and Administered by EMI VIRGIN MUSIC, INC.

THE SPIRIT OF RADIO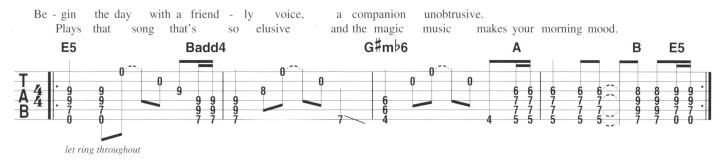

Alex Lifeson of Rush has made a career of add chords, sus chords, open chords moved around the neck, and yes, open-string barre chords, as in the verse to "The Spirit of Radio."

Be - gin   the day   with a friend - ly   voice,   a companion   unobtrusive.
Plays that   song   that's   so elusive   and the magic   music   makes your   morning mood.

DO YOU SLEEP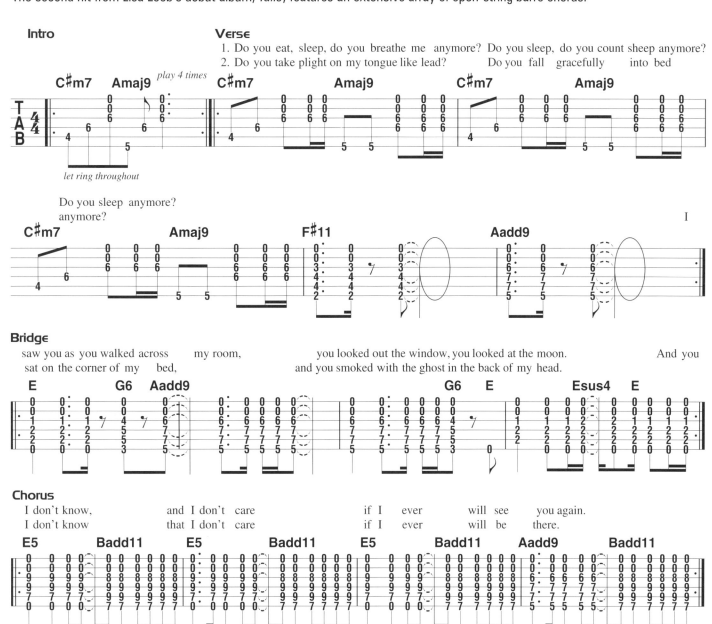

The second hit from Lisa Loeb's debut album, *Tails*, features an extensive array of open-string barre chords.

Intro

Verse

1. Do you eat, sleep, do you breathe me anymore? Do you sleep, do you count sheep anymore?
2. Do you take plight on my tongue like lead?   Do you fall   gracefully   into bed

Do you sleep anymore?
anymore?

Bridge

saw you as you walked across   my room,   you looked out the window, you looked at the moon.   And you
sat on the corner of my   bed,   and you smoked with the ghost in the back of my head.

Chorus

I don't know,   and I don't   care   if I   ever   will see   you again.
I don't know   that I don't   care   if I   ever   will be   there.

NO EXCUSES

Grunge rockers Alice in Chains struck paydirt with their acoustic side on this 1994 hit from their double-platinum album *Jar of Flies*. Play the intro part during the verses, which are arranged in lead sheet format here.

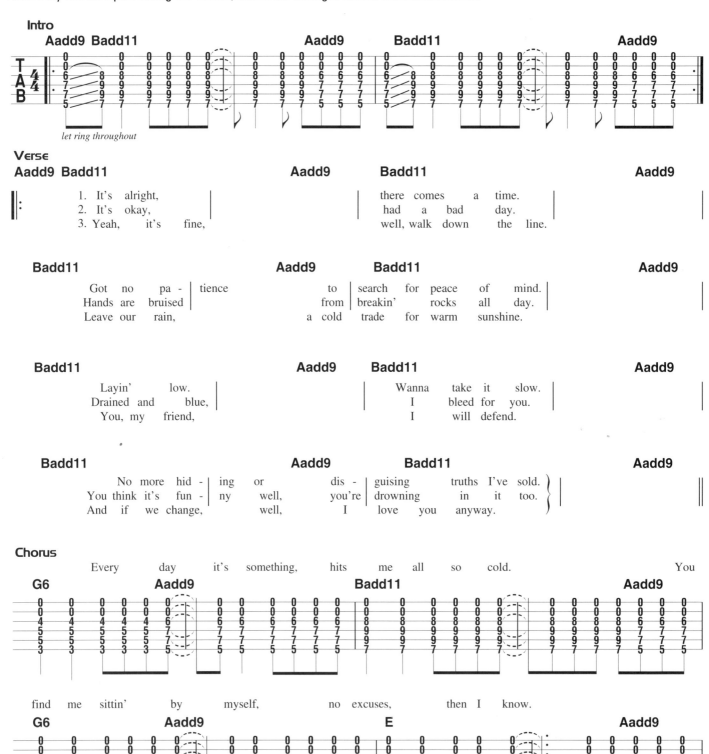

Verse

Aadd9 Badd11		Aadd9	Badd11		Aadd9
1. It's alright,		there comes	a time.		
2. It's okay,		had a	bad day.		
3. Yeah, it's fine,		well, walk down	the line.		

Badd11 ... **Aadd9** **Badd11** ... **Aadd9**

Got no pa - tience to search for peace of mind.
Hands are bruised from breakin' rocks all day.
Leave our rain, a cold trade for warm sunshine.

Badd11 ... **Aadd9** **Badd11** ... **Aadd9**

Layin' low. Wanna take it slow.
Drained and blue, I bleed for you.
You, my friend, I will defend.

Badd11 ... **Aadd9** **Badd11** ... **Aadd9**

No more hid - ing or dis - guising truths I've sold.
You think it's fun - ny well, you're drowning in it too.
And if we change, well, I love you anyway.

Chorus

Every day it's something, hits me all so cold. You

find me sittin' by myself, no excuses, then I know.

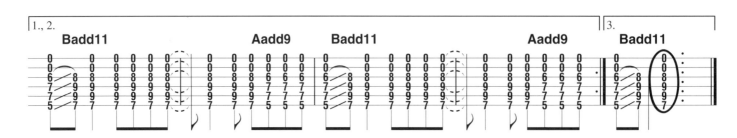

Written by Jerry Cantrell
Copyright © 1993 Buttnugget Publishing (ASCAP)